No Sweat

REAL ESTATE
INVESTING

High Returns · Low Risk · Zero Hassles

How to enjoy the profits
from owning revenue property
without the headache of dealing with
tenants and toilets.

No Sweat Real Estate Investing

ISBN-13:
ISBN-10:

Published by: Celebrity Expert Author
http://celebrityexpertauthor.com

Canadian Address:
501- 1155 The High Street,
Coquitlam, BC, Canada
V3B.7W4
Phone: (604) 941-3041
Fax: (604) 944-7993

US Address:
1300 Boblett Street
Unit A-218
Blaine, WA 98230
Phone: (866) 492-6623
Fax: (250) 493-6603

Dedication

This book is dedicated to the ever supporting love of my life, Tricia and our three amazing sons, Vincent, Aiden and Linden. Thank you for always believing in me and joining me on this wild and sometimes crazy journey.

Foreward

How Real Estate Investing Has Changed My Life

I thought it would be good to share my own personal story that has allowed me to create financial success for myself (and my investor partners) through real estate investing.

When I was just twenty four years old a friend of mine sent me a book called "Rich Dad, Poor Dad" (by Robert Kiyosaki) and that sparked my interest in real estate investing. At the time I was trading my time for money as an apprentice pipe-fitter. I was making pretty good money and trying to put some of it away – but it was tough to save diligently. This was even more true when the love of my life, Tricia told me that she was pregnant with our first son (we now have three).

With what I learned from the book, as well as some good advice from a friend, I bought two rental properties as well as our own first home.

Then one day on the dreary drive to work, I had a life-changing 'ah-ha' moment that I will always remember. I thought to myself "If I could just hold onto these three properties for 25 years, I would be able to retire early at the age of 50 and have a million dollars in equity as well as enough cash flow to bring in at least $60,000 per year to live on."

The properties would be free and clear and cashflowing like crazy.

At that point I realized that I'd stumbled upon a very good thing. I was hooked on this idea of buying properties and holding on to them for the long term.

I decided to focus on buying residential properties (single family homes and apartment buildings) and I chose Grande Prairie as the market to buy in. After some initial trial and error, I quickly developed my own unique 'niche'…providing FURNISHED rentals (or as I like to call them, "Super Suites"). By adding furniture to a rental unit, I was able to generate 2-3 times the PROFIT compared to the same property being unfurnished.

Thanks to investing in real estate, by age 27 I was able to quit my high-paying pipefitter j.o.b. and become a full-time real estate entrepreneur and stay-at-home dad.

Since then, together with my investor partners, I've created a multi-million dollar portfolio of over 70 rental units. My partners enjoy an above-average return on their money, along with a major growth in their net-worth.

Not only has real estate investing allowed me to create our dream life-style for my family and I, but it's also helping my investor partners to enjoy profits today, as well as long-term wealth.

I hope you enjoy reading this book as much as I've enjoyed working on it. When you are ready to start benefiting from my "No Sweat" investing strategy, please visit my website at **www.FreshCoastInvestments.ca** or give me a call at **780-882-3396**.

To your Real Estate Investing Success!

Aaron Bellmore

Table of Contents

Jim, a Real Estate Entrepreneur, meets Bill, a potential
Money-Partner.

Introduction

"Ninety percent of all millionaires become so through owning real estate."
—**Andrew Carnegie (the world's first billionaire)**

Welcome to *No-Sweat Real Estate Investing*. The title of this short book makes a rather large claim. It says that you can enjoy high returns with low risk and zero hassles.

The subtitle is "How to enjoy the profits from owning revenue property without the headache of dealing with tenants and toilets."

These are very bold statements, and it is the author's intention to give you an overview of how the business of real estate works, as well as how other people just like you are achieving amazing financial rewards thanks to investing in revenue properties.

Chances are you either know someone who has made a lot of money from a real estate deal or you have seen television shows where the host makes big profits 'flipping' a property. Perhaps you have even seen your own home increase in value over the years.

In the back of your head you may have wondered how you can get going in real estate and start profiting for yourself and your family. If you are like most people in today's busy, hectic world, you have probably been held back due to work and family obligations.

These responsibilities have prevented you from getting training for investing in real estate the right way. Or you may have received some training but not had the chance to actually get the ball rolling.

The purpose of this book is to give you a good overview of the ins and outs of real estate as an investment, and to show you how you can enjoy the benefits without the hassles of having to do it all yourself.

Throughout this book you will see the term *real estate entrepreneur*, as well as the terms *money partner* or *investor partner* (which mean the same thing), so it is important that we begin by clarifying these terms.

Why *real estate entrepreneur*? The origin of the word entrepreneur is French and it means "one who undertakes or manages." This means that as real estate entrepreneurs, we are the deal-makers who pull everything and everyone together to purchase and profit from a particular piece of property.

As a real estate entrepreneur, we are in the business of real estate investing. We have taken the training, gotten the experience, and we are actively pursuing and making deals regularly.

The money partner (or investor partner) has a much different role. They put up the funds and, in some cases, their credit worthiness to purchase the property.

Typically, that is the full extent of their involvement in the active portion of the transaction. This is why it is a hands-free investment for them. They are not involved in the day-to-day operations of the business (in other words, they don't have to deal with the "tenants and toilets").

In exchange for their financial backing, the money partner shares in the profits of the deal.

How to read this book

There are seven chapters in this book. You may read them in order, or jump around as you prefer. We have purposely kept this book short and to the point because it is meant to be more of a primer about real estate investing than step-by-step instructions. You should be able to read this entire book in one afternoon.

If, after reading it, you get excited about becoming an active real estate entrepreneur and you want more information about specific training programs, please feel free to reach out to the author, who will be happy to guide you to the best resources. (The author's contact information is on the back cover of this book.)

On the other hand, if you are like the majority of busy people, you would like to enjoy the benefits of real estate without the hassles of doing it yourself.

In that case, choosing the right real estate entrepreneur to join forces with you is very important. Please feel free to contact the author for a friendly chat, to find out more about their area of expertise, and to learn about the market they focus on.

All right, enough with the preamble... let's get going and take a look at the top 10 reasons for investing in real estate!

"The best investment on earth is earth."

Louis Glickman

Jim explains the Big Benefits of real estate as an investment.

Chapter 1:

Why Real Estate? Top 10 Reasons

M any people wonder why they should invest in real estate rather than place their money in the stock market, mutual funds, gold, silver, diamonds, or any other kind of investment.

Here are the top 10 reasons why real estate is better than all the other options listed above:

Reason #1:
The Wealthiest People Are Investing in Real Estate

Yes, it's true.

According to a recent report by MSNBC, the super-rich invest heavily in real estate, regardless of the market's volatility.

The reason is simple: Real estate is a proven, tangible asset which will continue to be valuable, especially as the world's population continues to grow. To put it simply: As long as people need shelter, real estate properties will be in high demand.

Reason #2:
Stability

As mentioned above, rich and savvy investors place their money in real estate whether the stock market—or economy in general—is up, down, or stagnant, as the real estate segment tends to remain stable.

Even if the price of properties goes down, the drop is not as drastic or sudden as is often the case with the stock market.

If the real estate market crashes—as was the case in the US in 2008—historically it has been proven over and over again that it will go back to its original value within four to six years. After that, its worth will continue to grow.

Real estate rebounds when other investments don't because while people can do without luxuries like gold or diamonds, they will always need shelter.

Reason #3:
Control

With most investments, you have no control or power over what happens. If you buy stocks or bonds, you are entrusting your money to the performance of a third party—a company—to create wealth for you over the long term, but you have zero control over how that business is being run.

If you invest in mutual funds, you trust the fund manager to select the appropriate stocks to create a good return for you. And if you opt for gold and silver, you again have no control over how these commodities will perform on the market.

With real estate, however, we can exercise a great deal of control. For instance, we can determine what market we will buy in and what kind of property we will purchase. We can even control the negotiation of the purchase of the property in order to get it at an undervalued price in the first place.

But there is more: We can control the condition of the property we purchase. This means that we can buy and increase the value of our real estate holdings by choosing underperforming properties and fixing them up. This way, they will be worth more money than what we originally purchased them for.

Our control also extends to the kind of financing we get, how long we choose to own the property, and when and how we choose to sell it.

That's not all! We can also control what kind of tenants we rent to, how our property is managed, and much more.

As you can see, with real estate investments we exercise much more control over our money than with other kinds of investments.

Reason #4: Leverage

When purchasing an income property, chances are we will be using the banks' money. We will come up with a down payment of anywhere from 15 to 25 percent of the property's value and the bank will finance the rest. This means we are using between 75 to 85 percent leverage on that property.

So for a relatively small amount of money— 15 to 25 percent of the total purchase price— we get to control the entire value (100 percent) of that property. No other investment allows you to do that.

Typically, if you want to purchase something, you have to pay the entire price. If, say, you want to buy one ounce of gold, you must pay for it in its entirety at whatever the current market price is.

With real estate, it's a totally different story.

If we bring in 20 percent down, the bank puts in 80 percent. Yet—and this is a *huge* advantage—we control and own 100 percent of that property. We also benefit from all the different profit centers on that property, even though we invested only a small sum.

So that is leverage, which is one of the reasons why real estate is so incredibly attractive to smart investors.

Reason #5:
Price Flexibility

One of the beautiful things about investing in real estate is that the price is flexible.

This means that everything is negotiable when it comes to real estate investing. Usually, the property's listed price is not what an astute investor will actually pay for it. A professional investor will negotiate and get the best deal possible, getting a reduction in the price and/or favorable terms for purchasing the property.

This is in stark contrast to what happens with other investments. If you are trying to buy gold and silver, for example, the price is the price. There is no wiggle room, and no negotiations are possible. The same holds true for stocks, bonds, and mutual funds. The price you see is the price you pay.

So real estate investing is attractive because the price is flexible.

Reason #6:
Demand Is Outstripping Supply

In the North American real estate market, supply and demand is in the investors' favor.

That's very good news because in most markets, the demand for rental properties outstrips the available supply.

One of the main reasons for this situation is the cost of constructing new rental units versus what can be charged for rent.

Over the last several decades, many apartment buildings have been converted into condominiums, putting an even greater squeeze on the rental markets. This means fewer rental units and more renters looking for them.

So when we choose to buy real estate, the supply-and-demand factor is definitely in our favor.

Reason #7:
Other People Pay for Your Investment

One of the great things about owning rental properties is that over time, our tenants are actually paying for the investment.

How does this work? It's very simple.

When we buy an investment property, we have to come up with the down payment and get a mortgage on that property. Then we make monthly mortgage payments to the bank.

Fortunately, when our tenants pay us rent, they are actually paying off our loan at the

the same time. Any money left over after the loan payment, insurance, property taxes, and other expenses is our profit!

So not only are other people paying for our investment, but if we are earning income from that property, our tenants are also paying us an excellent cash-on-cash return on the investment!

Reason #8:
The Value of Real Estate Continues to Grow Even Once You Are Retired

Think about it: Government-sponsored retirement plans or tax-deferred programs are designed so that the amount of money you receive actually decreases over time. Plus, you are taxed. If you invest in these plans or programs, then when you are elderly and may need extra cash, chances are there won't be any money left.

Real estate is completely different: the lon-ger you hold on to it, the more money you will end up with. You'll pay down or pay off the loan on the property, which will generate more cash flow from the property itself. You also have the option to refinance properties and pull out your equity (by way of a loan), tax-free!

So unlike government-sponsored retirement plans, real estate actually increases your net worth and cash flow over time. You may even enjoy some significant tax advantages as well.

Isn't it important to you to make more money and enjoy a good lifestyle as you get older? This question may sound like a no-brainer, but it all comes down to your investment choices. Real estate allows you to have a good life and actually increase your income as you get older (which is when you will most need it).

Reason #9:
Property Is a Tangible Asset

Real estate is made up of land and buildings—tangible, touchable assets.

Even if the economy tanked, you would still have the land and the structure as a solid asset.

Compare this with other investments like stocks and bonds. These are basically promissory notes put out by a company saying that the company will do its best to live up to its obligations and increase the value of the company.

Unfortunately, if something goes wrong—as it did back in 2008—the value of the company can diminish very quickly. Or, in the worst-case scenario, the company can disappear altogether, along with the value of your stocks, bonds, or mutual funds.

Not so with real estate. Even in bad times real estate would still be an asset, for all the reasons listed above. People will always need a roof over their heads.

Reason #10:
You Can Pass Real Estate On to Your Kids

When you buy and hold real estate as an investment, you can pass it on to your heirs.

Compare this to a company- or government-sponsored pension plan. Which option do you think is better?

You might be able to pass the company pension plan on to your spouse, but that is as far as that will go.

Real estate, however, can be passed down from generation to generation. That is exactly what many of the wealthiest families have done and continue to do year after year.

Chapter 1 Summary:

As you can see, there are many reasons why real estate is a better choice for investing than other investment vehicles. The rich put their money in real estate because it is a much more stable investment.

It also gives you control over your money, you can use other people's cash for massive leverage, the investment continues to grow even when you are retired, it is a tangible investment that fills a basic human need (shelter), and last but certainly not least, you can pass it on to your loved ones.

In chapter two, we will to look into the specific ways you can make money from investing in real estate. You will be surprised and delighted by how many profit centers there are!

"Real estate is the best investment in the world because it is the only thing they're not making anymore."

Will Rogers

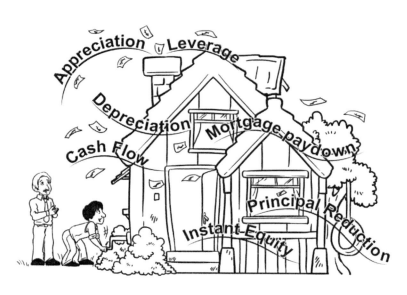

Jim shows Bill how the money is made with real estate.

Chapter 2:

The Multiple Profit Centers of Real Estate

R eal estate is a fantastic investment for many different reasons. We went over 10 of those reasons in the previous chapter.

Now let's look at seven specific profit centers whereby you can make money in real estate.

Profit Center #1:
Instant Equity

Instant equity is created when we purchase a property for less than its true market value, which savvy investors always try to do.

Now, you might be asking yourself, How is that possible? Why would anybody sell their property for less than it's worth?

This is a good question. The answer is that people have different, personal reasons to sell their property at a discount. Maybe they are going through a divorce or moving out of the area. Or perhaps they inherited the property and don't want to keep it. It could also be—and, in fact, often is—that the owners are facing some financial dificulties requiring them to liquidate the property.

In all these cases, the property owners must make a quick sale and are thus not focusing on getting top dollar for it. That, of course, is to our advantage because it enables us, the buyer, to purchase a property for a better price.

That is how we gain instant equity, which virtually guarantees us a profit when we sell the property or refinance it in the future.

Having instant equity also provides a buf- fer in case of emergencies. So if there is a problem with the property down the road, that instant equity can be a big help.

Profit Center #2: Leverage

We mentioned leverage in Chapter 1; now let's dig deeper into how, exactly, it works and why it is considered a profit center in real estate.

As a reminder, we can typically buy invest- ment properties with a down payment of 15 to 25 percent of the total price, with the bank financing the rest.

How does that turn into a profit center? It's a thing of beauty!

As the property increases in value (appre- ciates)—which is another one of the profit centers we'll talk about shortly—its worth grows based on the entire value of the property.

For example, if we have a $400,000 property and it goes up in value by 5 percent in one year, we'll end up with a $20,000 increase and a 5 percent total appreciation.

Those are the figures, but if we look at leverage, our return on the investment is actually much, much higher than that.

Let's say we put a down payment of 25 percent on that $400,000 property. That would be a $100,000 cash investment in the deal. The bank then finances $300,000, for the total $400,000 purchase price.

Now when we look at our return on investment from leverage, it's much higher because that 5 percent appreciation, or $20,000 in increased value in a year, is actually $20,000 return on our initial $100,000 cash investment.

As if by magic, the 5 percent increase in the property value is actually a 20 percent return on the money invested. That is the power of leverage.

Think about it: You are actually making money on the bank's investment! That is why leverage is such a powerful profit center.

Profit Center #3: Cash Flow

Cash flow is the money that is left over at the end of the month after we have paid all of the expenses on a property: the mortgage, property taxes, insurance, management, and maintenance.

If, for instance, we are charging $1,000 a month in rent and our total expenses add up to $900 a month, our cash flow is $100 per month.

There are several different ways to increase the cash flow. One of them is to minimize the expenses on the property, and another is to pay down the mortgage as quickly as possible.

Typically, the mortgage is the largest expense on a property. When we pay off a big chunk of it (or, even better, pay it off completely), that will increase our cash flow exponentially.

Another way of getting more cash flow is to own more rental units in a specific property. For example, a small apartment building with several rental units would generate more income than a single-family home with just one rental unit and source of income.

There are several more creative strategies that can help increase cash flow. You will learn about them in later chapters.

Remember: Cash flow is king, so we always want to make sure that we have positive cash flow. It goes without saying that we want to avoid paying for the property after we've bought it; it should be paying us.

Profit Center #4:
Mortgage Pay-Down

As mentioned before, we can reduce the mortgage owing so that the bank loan is reduced every month.

Mortgage pay-down is similar to instant equity, leverage, and appreciation in that it is a kind of hidden profit center.

Why hidden? Because we do not benefit from it directly until we either sell the property or refinance it, although it definitely does make your net worth statement look very nice.

Now let's take a closer look at what makes up a typical mortgage payment. Mortgage payments are comprised of two components: interest and principal.

When we first get the loan, most of our mortgage payment actually goes toward paying down the interest on the loan. As we get closer to the end of the mortgage term, most of the money will go toward the principal part of the loan.

This is called amortization. This is the sneaky way that the banks can make very, very good money, even with interest rates as low as 2-3 percent. In a nutshell, they charge us most of that interest up front in the first one-third to one half of the mortgage term.

One of the strategies for increasing the mortgage pay-down is to make additional payments that count toward payment of the principal portion of the loan only. This helps reduce the principal owed much faster than by just making regular payments.

This is where our tenant comes in. Every month that our tenant pays the rent, they are helping us lower our mortgage balance little by little.

Over time, this payout becomes very substantial. It is another profit center that we see in real estate that does not exist in other investments.

Profit Center #5: Appreciation

Appreciation is the natural increase in the value of a property over time.

If you were lucky enough to buy a home in a major city 30 years ago for $30,000 or $40,000, today your property may be worth as much as $1,000,000. That is huge appreciation.

Of course, different markets have different appreciation rates. And don't forget that real estate is cyclical. This means that sometimes appreciation is aggressive and high, while at other times it is meek and low. In the worst-case scenario, it can be flat or even negative.

Generally speaking, however, property values go up over time, usually increasing at a higher rate than inflation.

You probably heard about people buying a property and flipping it soon after, making $30,000 or even as much as $100,000 in profit because the market was very hot.

While it may sound great, this strategy is risky, so beware. This is pure speculation, as the investors are relying solely on fast market appreciation to make their money. However, if that particular market goes flat or negative, most speculators will go broke because they have set up their investment so that it is completely reliant on just this one profit center.

Pure speculation is not what smart investors do.

Remember: The advantage of appreciation is that it is reliable *over time*. Investors who make the biggest profit from appreciation

tend to be the ones who buy and hold properties for five years or longer.

You may know the saying, "Good things
come to those who wait!" A good one for real
estate investing is, "Don't wait to buy real estate.
Buy real estate and wait."

Profit Center #6: Reinvestment

Reinvestment is when you take the profits from one real estate venture and then use
them to buy another real estate investment.

Let's say you own a property for five
years and then you refinance it and take out
$100,000 in profit. If you use that $100,000 to
buy another property, then you are reinvesting.

Reinvesting is a great way of using your
money to create even more wealth for yourself and your family.

Profit Center #7:
Depreciation

Earlier on, we mentioned all the benefits of appreciation. Now let's talk about its opposite: depreciation. This is a tax-reduction strategy that some investors like to use as another way of creating income from their real estate properties.

In a nutshell, depreciation means that the government is allowing us to lower our taxes because (in theory, at least) the value of the structure on the land decreases over time. The building itself deteriorates with wear and tear, and eventually it will need to be replaced.

The government understands this and allows us to depreciate the structure by a certain percentage every year. This means we can take off that amount from the total income generated by the building (and per- haps even from your personal income) and use it as a tax savings.

The problem with depreciation, however, is that what the government gives, the government also takes away.

So while it is true that the condition of the structure does decrease over time, the value of the entire property typically goes up at a much higher rate.

Imagine this scenario: You take depreciation benefits, but when you sell the property for more than what you paid for it (which is by far the usual case), the government claws back any tax refunds it gave you as depreciation.

The bottom line is this: Depreciation makes sense for some investors, depending on their particular income level and financial situation.

It tends to make more sense the longer you plan on holding the property. In fact, if you keep the property indefinitely, it is probably a very wise strategy. On the other hand, if you only plan on owning the property for five years or less, depreciation may not be a good idea.

This is something that varies from investor to investor, so you need to discuss your unique financial situation with a qualified financial professional, such as an accountant.

Chapter 2 Summary:

Unlike other investment classes that typically offer one or perhaps two different ways to make money, with real estate, there are seven!

We can create instant equity and buy a property for less than its true value. We can use leverage with the bank financing the majority of the purchase price of a property while we enjoy profits on the entire value of that property.

Cash flow is the net profit that is left over every month after we pay all of the expenses.

With the mortgage we (or better said, our tenants) pay down, we pay off the loan little by little and increase our equity in the property over time.

Appreciation is the natural increase in market value of the property over time.

Reinvestment is using the profits we make from one property to buy another, ideally increasing our cash flow and net worth at the same time.

And depreciation is a tax reduction or deferral strategy that makes sense for some investors depending on their particular financial situation and the length of time they will be holding the property.

In the next chapter, let's take a look at the different styles and kinds of real estate investments that are available to you. There is a veritable buffet of different choices.

"Don't wait to buy real estate,
buy real estate and wait."
T. Harv Eker

"Real estate investing, even on a very small scale, remains a tried and true means of building an individual's cash flow and wealth."
Robert Kiyosaki

"Landlords grow rich in their sleep."
John Stuart

"Real estate cannot be lost or stolen, nor can it be carried away. Purchased with common sense, paid for in full, and managed with reasonable care, it is about the safest investment in the world."
Franklin D. Roosevelt

"If you're not going to put your money in real estate, where else?"
Tamir Sapir

Jim explains the many different styles
of real estate investing.

Chapter 3:

The Different Styles of Real Estate Investing

One of the most attractive things about real estate—besides its profit-earning potential, of course—is that it offers a variety of different ways to invest in properties.

In this chapter, we will go over the seven most common real estate investment strategies a smart investor should definitely know about. The strategies are listed in no particular order of importance.

This is a quick overview. If you are interested in any one particular strategy, spend some time exploring it further.

Let's get started.

Strategy #1: Development

This strategy involves buying a piece of raw land and building on it. With this option, you don't just purchase a ready-made house; you build it yourself. (We don't mean you actually have to do any work yourself—unless you are qualified to do so, of course. You can hire professionals.)

This could be any type of property: a single-family home, multi-family dwelling, commercial property, or mixed-use commercial and residential building. It all depends on what you are in the market for.

Development can be a very lucrative way to invest in real estate from the ground up. But there is a downside to this strategy as well:

it is the riskiest and most expensive strategy, and one that requires the most skill.

You not only have to know the local real estate market very well, but you also must be able to hire and oversee contractors, negotiate the best possible prices on supplies, understand how zoning and permits work in the municipality in which you are building, line up millions in financing, and know how to market your development for top dollar.

Development can be a very lucrative business, as the profits in a hot market can be outstanding. On the other hand, developers tend to be the first to bust in a market downturn, as they are so exposed financially.

The rewards can be very high, but so is the risk.

Strategy #2:
Buy, Fix, & Sell (Flip)

Flips are probably the best-known style of investing, featured in several TV programs that focus on this particular strategy.

The concept is that you buy a run-down property on the cheap, fix it up as quickly and inexpensively as possible, and then sell it at full market value (or as close to it as possible). If you are a handy person, this strategy might be right up your alley. It's exciting to hunt for and find a deal, break down walls with a sledgehammer, and see a whole new house emerge from the rubble.

If you can then sell the property quickly and make good money on it, this strategy will work well for you. But keep in mind that it could also be a risky undertaking: if you make a mistake in the initial purchase and the renovation costs you a lot more than you expected, or if you don't sell the house quickly, then you won't make as much profit as you had anticipated.

Flipping property is a short-term, appreciation-based investment strategy. The profits per deal tend to be lower than longer-term buy-and-hold deals, but this is offset by the number of deals that can be done in a relatively short time.

Still, many investors swear by this strategy and do many successful flips each year.

As in any real estate investing strategy, if you are prepared, well educated, and have a great team around you, you can be very successful with this tactic.

Strategy #3:
Single-Family Home Rentals

Next to flips, this is probably the most recognized style of real estate investing because it's so simple and easy to understand.

With this strategy, you buy a house and rent it out to a tenant. There are many pros to this kind of real estate investing. The biggest one is the sheer number of single-family homes on the market.

It's also a very desirable rental because most families prefer to rent a house rather than an apartment—it provides more space and more privacy.

It's also the kind of property that the banks are very happy to finance.

However, the challenge with single-family home rentals is getting positive cash flow from them. Typically, these houses are the most expensive kind of rental properties to purchase because you are buying a structure plus the building lot that it's sitting on.

Quite often, the amount of rent that you can charge will only cover your hard costs, such as your mortgage payment, property taxes, insurance, management, and maintenance. At the end of the month, there may not be anything left over for cash flow.

In fact, as rental properties, single-family homes are often cash flow negative.

There are, however, ways to get around this. The most common is to build a basement suite, turning one property into two rental units.

Strategy #4:
Rent-to-Own (Lease Options)

This is a creative strategy that goes like this: instead of just renting a single-family home, you lease it to a tenant and give the option to purchase the property at a specified time and price in the future.

With this strategy, you can typically charge above the market rent rate and get the tenants to take care of all the maintenance and upkeep on the property. Usually, the tenants will be motivated to do this since the house will eventually will be theirs.

The advantage of this strategy is that you can create a lot more cash flow than normal from a single-family home. Also, at the beginning of the lease you can get a deposit that's much higher than a usual damage deposit on a property.

Plus, there are usually fewer tenant management headaches with the rent-to-own strategy than with traditional rentals, because tenants are motivated and agree in their lease to take good care of the property.

However, there are some challenges with this strategy as well. The bulk of your profit is based on appreciation of the property. Not all rent-to-own deals work out as initially planned, with either the tenant backing out of the deal or the market not cooperating with the final price that you had agreed upon.

Also, rent-to-owns are usually short-term deals, lasting from two to four years. After that, you will need to find another property in order to keep your real estate investing business going.

Strategy #5:
Multi-Family Properties
(Apartment Buildings)

Traditionally, multi-family properties are two units or more. If you have a single-family home with a basement suite, it would be a multi-family property.

The banks consider anything more than four units as a commercial residential property. The financing rules and regulations change for that class of investment.

The advantages of multi-family homes are many. First of all, you have a much better eficiency of scale. So instead of having one rental unit with its own roof, furnace, hot water system, etc., you have multiple rental units under one roof all sharing the same heating system, water system, etc.

Due to the greater eficiencies, your revenues and cash flow per unit tend to be higher, and your cost per unit is much lower than with single-family properties.

You also benefit from the eficiencies of management. This means that if you had, say, a 12-unit apartment building instead of 12 properties in 12 different areas of town, you would have just one property to manage. The challenge of multi-family property investing is that it can be a bit more dificult to get financing for these kinds of buildings. Also, finding good deals may not be easy because there are fewer of them compared to single-family homes.

Strategy #6:
Commercial Properties

Strip malls, ofice buildings, commercial bays, and other buildings that house businesses all fall under the category of commercial properties.

As with any strategy, there are pros and cons you should know about before you decide to pursue this option. The big advantage of commercial real estate is that the tenants tend to pay higher rent and they are responsible for more of the expenses associated with the property.

The rent you charge is often based on what is called triple net. This means that the tenant is not just responsible for paying rent, but also for all of the utilities and property taxes as well. And quite often, the tenant also makes any improvements that are needed for their particular business.

Commercial tenants usually sign long-term leases and guarantee those leases personally.

So once you get a commercial tenant who has a successful business, that tenant will probably stick around for a long time, requiring very little management and maintenance. Now let's look at the challenges. The main one is that when commercial properties become vacant, especially during an economic downturn, they may remain unoccupied for a very, very long time. This means, of course, that you get no cash flow from that property and have to pay for all of the associated expenses out of your own pocket.

If you are interested in buying commercial properties, make sure that you really understand how this sector works. You may even benefit, at least initially, from investing with somebody who is a true expert in that area.

Strategy #7:
Tax Lien Certificates & Tax Deeds

This particular investment strategy is primarily used in the United States. Tax liens and tax deeds are a way for the local municipal governments to collect on unpaid taxes from property owners.

In the case of tax deeds, if a homeowner has been delinquent on their property taxes for a set period of time, the municipal government can take the property and auction it off. The property will go to the bidder who pays the overdue taxes.

In the case of tax lien certificates, the municipality (or county) will auction off the tax bill. The bids are based on how much interest the bidder wants to receive.

When the property owner eventually pays their taxes, they will be charged a penalty on top of delinquent taxes. The back taxes plus the penalty are then paid to the investor who bought that particular tax lien certificate.

If the property owner does not pay taxes within a specified period of time, the investor may then foreclose on the property and take legal ownership of it (quite often for just pennies on the dollar). Over 95 percent of the time, the taxes and penalties are paid in full and the investor enjoys a nice return on the money, which is backed by the local government.

Tax deeds are the same, except that by paying all of the back taxes and the penalties to the government, the investor actually ends up owning the property free and clear!

Each municipality has its own rules and regulations about exactly how this works. Different states are either tax lien or tax deed states. A few states are both.

Either way, this is an opportunity to literally buy properties for a fraction of what they are truly worth.

The important thing to know about tax liens and tax deeds is that you must do proper due diligence on the property you are going to bid on. That way, you're making sure that if you do end up owning it outright, you actually want it and it is worth what you paid for it.

This strategy has some challenges. For example, different municipalities may have different rules about this process, so it would be wise for you to focus on one particular area and get to know it really well.

Again, if you are interested in this strategy, get educated or work with a real estate entrepreneur who fully understands tax liens and tax deeds.

Chapter 3 Summary:

Seven of the most common investment strategies in real estate include developing a property from scratch and building new structures on it.

Then there is the buy, fix, and sell (flip) option, single-family home rentals, a rent-to-own strategy, multi-family properties, commercial properties, and tax liens and tax deeds.

In the next chapter, we will talk about all the steps involved in purchasing a property either alone or with investment partners.

If you need further information about any of the strategies outlined in this chapter, or you would like to find out about the author's preferred strategy, please see the contact information located on the back cover of this book.

Real estate investing is a complex team activity. In the following two chapters, we will dive into what's involved in doing a deal, and who we want to have on our team.

There's a LOT involved for a real estate entrepreneur
to put a deal together.

Chapter 4:

The Art of the Deal

I n this chapter, we will take a look at all of the moving parts that are required to make a real estate deal work. Before we start exploring what we have to know and do when purchasing a property, let's talk about people whose financial resources we may need in order to buy more or bigger deals. These people are called investment or money partners.

Not every real estate entrepreneur needs money partners. If they are financially able to invest alone, that's great—they won't have to split their profit with anyone. On the other hand, chances are they will run out of money and/or credit very quickly, and their portfolio will be small and stagnant.

Sharing the profits with investor partners allows us to grow our portfolio much bigger and faster than we could on our own.

Astute real estate entrepreneurs understand that it is much better to own half of a property and share in the profits rather than own 100 percent of nothing!

In this kind of partnership, the roles are clearly defined: the money partner provides the money and/or credit to obtain financing, while the real estate entrepreneur brings their expertise in finding, buying, and managing profitable properties.

Any income from the venture is divided either 50-50 or according to a fair and clear agreement between the parties.

This chapter pertains to both scenarios: Real estate entrepreneurs who go solo, as well as those who work with money partners.

There are many things a real estate entrepreneur must do in order to buy the best possible property—one that will generate the best
possible return on investment. Let's begin.

Step #1:
Searching for the Right Investment
Property

Finding the deal is done in many ways. The
most common one is through a real estate
agent. Agents have access to the Multiple
Listing Service (MLS) and can easily search
for the specific kind of property that the real
estate entrepreneur wants.

Although this is the easiest and most con-
venient way to find properties, it does not
usually lead to the best deals. That's because
everyone can see what is on the MLS, so the
really good deals don't stay available for very
long.

Fortunately, there are many proactive ways
to find deals. This includes putting up signs,
advertising in newspapers, sending direct

mail, scouting different properties, or hiring so-called bird dogs—individuals who will scout properties for us.

The Internet is a wonderful resource as well, with many different online classified ads on sites such as Craigslist, MLS, and numerous other sites that have real estate search engines.

But before we actually make an offer on a property we are interested in buying, we must investigate the current market conditions and prices of other similar properties in the neighborhood.

Also, if the house needs any improvements, we need to calculate the cost of fixing it up to see whether potential renters would offset our costs. Remember: This is an investment, so it should generate income for us.

Step #2:
Making Offers

We found the property we like, and now it's time to make the deal. This process involves writing the initial offer and negotiating favorable terms with the seller.

Making offers is a multi-faceted skill set which involves a lot of negotiating. Part of this process is having the property inspected by a professional so we know what, exactly, we are getting into before we close the deal.

Let's say the property needs a lot of work. At this point, we have three options: 1) walk away, 2) ask the owners to make the necessary repairs, or 3) renegotiate the initial deal and get the price reduced.

Step #3:
Getting the Financing Lined Up

Nowadays, the banks and other lending institutions require a lot of information and paperwork from their borrowers. So we have to get all our ducks in a row before applying for mortgage.

The financing should match our needs and goals, as well as those of our money partners.

Step #4:
Setting Up the Proper Legal Structure for the Deal

Depending on the type and size of the deal, there are many different ways to set it up legally between the real estate entrepreneur and the money partners.

This could be anything from a joint venture agreement to a co-tenancy agreement to setting up a separate corporation.

The way this is done depends on the kind of property we are purchasing, the financing structure, and the final exit strategy.

As with any investment venture, it is important that you get professional legal and accounting advice as to what best serves you.

Step #5:
Handling the Day-to-Day Operation of the Property Once the Purchase Is Completed

Congratulations, we now own an investment property! This is a good time to plan

tasks such as maintenance and repairs, paint-
ing, landscaping, and taking care of any tenant
problems that may arise.

Step #6:
Reporting on the Progress to Investor
Partners

If we have investor partners, it is our
responsibility to keep them up to speed on
how the deal is rolling along. That includes
keeping proper records of all income and
expenses, as well as creating easy-to-under-
stand reports and financial statements on a
regular basis. (By the way, the jurisdiction or
municipality where the property is located
will also require proper documentation.)

This on-going communication with our
money partners is necessary to make sure that
everybody is on the same page and knows
what's going on, but without bogging anyone
down with excessive details.

This is about developing that delicate balance between providing great information

and providing too much information. (Of course, the super-analytical investor partners may actually like to be bogged down by piles of data!)

Step #7:
Finalizing the Deal for a Smooth & Profitable Exit

This involves marketing and selling (or refinancing) the property for the maximum value with the minimum cost. Again, depending on the style of investment and everyone's objectives, this may be a short-term real estate transaction—something in the three to six months range. It could also be a medium-term venture, lasting between one and five years. Or, it could perhaps be a longer deal: say, five or more years.

Whatever the timeframe, the focus should be on maximizing the return on investment for our partners and ourselves. Likewise, we should have a good exit plan: is the property going to be sold for a profit or is it going to be refinanced?

Whatever option we choose, everything must be done properly from both a legal and an accounting point of view.

If we have investment partners, we need to provide them with a simple statement of account that can be used for their tax returns at the end of the year.

As you can see, a real estate entrepreneur has many responsibilities.

Now, let's look at what the roles and responsibilities of the money partner are.

First of all, the money partner must decide if a particular deal is the right fit for them or not.

This step involves getting independent legal and financial advice, as well as doing their own due diligence about the real estate entrepreneur with whom they are going to be investing.

Questions money partners should ask are: Does this deal meet my financial requirements, either short- or long-term? Am I comfortable with the level of risk involved? Do I understand the pros and cons of the particular investment strategy and the market I will be investing in?

So there you have it: all the steps that a real estate entrepreneur needs to take in order to find, buy, and close the deal—whether alone or with a money partner.

"Ninety percent of all millionaires become so through owning real estate."

Andrew Carnegie

Chapter 4 Summary:

Let's review. The process involves:

- looking for properties through various ofline and online sources,

- getting the proper inspections and nego-tiating the price and terms of the pur-chase,

- obtaining the financing,

- setting up the legal framework,

- managing and maintaining the property,

- reporting progress to money partners, and

- making plans for an exit or refinancing strategy.

In the next chapter, we will look at the different professionals who help an entrepreneur buy and manage an investment property.

In the meantime, if you have further questions about the material covered in this chapter, please contact the author by using the contact info on the back cover of this book.

It's important to work with a good TEAM.

Chapter 5:

Building Your Winning Team

I n the previous chapter, we talked about finding and purchasing an investment property. There are many important steps involved in this process, and you may be wondering whether you can do all this work by yourself.

If you have the time, inclination, and ability to take care of many things on your own (in other words, if you are a Jack- or Jill-of-all-trades), then you can do some of it, but you can never do *all* of it completely by yourself.

The reality is that no one can be good at everything that is involved in finding, organizing, and managing a real estate deal.

A real estate entrepreneur's time is best used by creating and managing an effective team and then doing deals—rather than trying to do everything alone.

With that in mind, let's take a look at what is involved in creating our winning real estate investment team. In this chapter, we will look at the experts who can help us with each step, as well as what their individual roles and responsibilities are.

Assembling the Power Team

Successful real estate investing is definitely a team sport, not just a one-person show. It requires the input and the help of many different professionals, including a realtor or real estate agent.

A real estate agent's role is to both help us find properties *and* sell them for us when we are ready to do so.

A good realtor can also be very helpful with negotiations and making sure that the paperwork for our deals is in order.

The next member on our team is a mortgage broker—in other words, the finance specialist. This person shops the market for the best financing for our deals, prepares the paperwork, and presents it to different lending institutions in order for us to get the ideal loan for the property.

One advantage of working with the mortgage broker is that they don't work for any one particular bank. Instead, this person will scout around and find the best financing for our particular situation.

Typically, for single-family properties, the mortgage broker gets paid by the lending institution. But for multi-family and commercial properties, we will have to pay the mortgage broker's fee.

The next member of our team should be a financial professional (a bookkeeper and/ or accountant) who has experience with real estate deals. A financial professional will keep our books in order and make sure that our tax bill is as low as possible and that the taxes we do owe actually get paid.

We will also need a real estate appraiser to determine what the true value of a given property is and to ensure that we are not over-paying for it.

This is important not only for us as the deal-maker but also for the bank, since it doesn't want to loan us more money than the property is actually worth.

An insurance specialist is also an import-ant part of our team and will obtain the cor-rect insurance plan for the property—a plan that covers fires, earthquakes, floods, and other natural disasters.

Those are the most obvious kinds of insur-ance that we will need for the property in case a catastrophy occurs. However, there are also some lesser-known insurance policies that are important as well, such as liability insur-ance (which protects us in case the tenant or somebody else gets hurt on the property).

There is also loss of revenue insurance. If something were to happen to the property, it might take a long time to fix it. In the meantime, this kind of insurance will cover not only our mortgage payments and expenses, but also our net income from the property, so we are not losing all of the cash flow.

Now let's talk about legal experts and the role they play on our team. When purchasing the property, we want to make sure that everything is done legally and above board.

It's important that each person—not just the buyer and seller, but also any investment partners involved—has access to their own independent legal advice. This way, everyone's interests are represented fairly. This legal paperwork should outline such details as how the deal is going to be structured, what each party is responsible for, etc.

We will also need some good suppliers on our team.

If we are involved with the construction or renovation, we will need people who can sell us furniture, appliances, and other equipment for our properties. If we establish a good relationship with these suppliers, chances are we will get better pricing and service from them.

Depending on the kind of property we are buying, we may have to use one or more property inspectors.

These professionals are very important for several reasons. First of all, we want to make sure that we go into the deal with our eyes wide open as to what the current and potential challenges with that property are.

Therefore, we must ensure that we have a very knowledgeable property inspector who will go through the property with a fine-toothed comb to detect all of the problem areas that might exist.

This is also a very good way to be able to renegotiate the purchase price: if the inspector finds any problems with the building, we can either ask that they be dealt with by current owners before we buy the property, or get a discount so we can take care of those issues ourselves.

More team members include maintenance and construction specialists.

These professionals—construction workers, plumbers, heat and air-conditioning installers, etc.—are very important if we are planning on building or renovating houses.

We will also need property management professionals.

Once we find and buy a property, we will need someone to manage it. The property manager will be responsible for finding tenants, as well as maintaining the property.

As you can see, each of the above-mentioned professionals has a clearly defined role. Together, they will form a power team that will make sure our investment is in good hands.

Questions about this chapter? Don't hesitate to contact the author by using the contact information on the back cover of this book.

Chapter 5 Summary:

Purchasing and managing a successful investment property requires the help of many professionals with different roles and responsibilities.

A power team usually consists of a realtor or real estate agent, mortgage broker, financial professional (a bookkeeper and/or accountant), a real estate appraiser, insurance specialist, inspector, legal expert, suppliers, maintenance and construction specialists, and property management professionals.

As wonderful as real estate investing is, it also has some risks and drawbacks involved.

In the next chapter, we will look at some of the most common challenges associated with real estate, as well as some solutions. This way, you will be fully aware of both the opportunities and the potential downsides.

"Buying real estate is not only the best way, the quickest way, the safest way, but the only way to become wealthy."

Marshall Field

"Real estate investing has created more millionaires than any other form of investing because of its many advantages. Whether you are investing for cash flow or capital gains..."

Robert Kiyosaki

.

Chapter 6:

The Risks of
Real Estate Investing

So far in this book, we have talked about the advantages of real estate investing. First, we looked at all the reasons why real estate is such an incredible investment choice compared to other options.

Second, we looked at the different profit centers of real estate investing. Then we went on to see various styles and a variety of real estate investing techniques.

In the last two chapters, we discussed the process of deal-making, the roles and responsibilities of the real estate entrepreneur and the money partner, as well as various professionals who make up our power team and can help with the property purchase, financing, and maintenance.

As with any investment, it is important that you go into this venture with your eyes wide open. In this chapter, we are going to look at several of the most common risks associated with real estate investing and some of the possible solutions to those challenges.

Risk #1:
The Real Estate Market Could Crash

This is probably the biggest fear many novice investors have about real estate, especially since the memory of the 2008 housing meltdown in the United States is still fresh in our minds.

This is an understandable concern, considering that in several regions of the US, property prices dropped by as much as 50 percent in 12 to 24 months.

The reality is that the real estate crisis affected only five main markets. The rest of the country was largely unaffected with regards to falling property prices. They didn't see the kind of appreciation they had prior to the crisis, but these markets did not crash, either.

An important thing to remember is that real estate follows a predictable cycle of rising prices, plateau, and decline, which then repeats.

History and experience shows that the only time you should really be concerned about housing market adjustments or crashes is if you are in a very short-term investment strategy.

But if you take a long-term approach to real estate investing and you focus on more than just appreciation as a profit center, then these normal market ups and downs will not have as much impact on you.

The bottom line is this: If the market you are investing in declines but you hold the property for several years, the values will come up to where they were before—and then the prices will continue to increase. So the fear of the housing market crash is a justified concern only if you are in a short-term strategy.

Risk #2:
The Rental Market Could Go Down

This is a consideration if the local area you are investing in experiences some sort of dramatic economic change and many people leave the area. Or it could be a concern if you are in an area that gets overbuilt with rental units.

Although the rental market could go down, it is—just like property values we mentioned above—a cyclical phenomenon.

In the short term, the rent may have to be lowered in order to keep the vacancy rate low.

But in the long term, you should be able to get on track again within a couple of years.

There are several different ways to mitigate this risk. If you focus on single-family homes, you could consider adding a basement suite, as well as possibly renting out the garage separately. This would turn a single-family home rental into two or even three different revenue streams (thereby increasing your cash flow and decreasing your risk exposure if one unit is vacant).

With multi-family properties, you could consider adding incentives such as free utilities, flat-screen TVs, and lower rent when tenants sign on for a minimum one-year lease.

As far as determining if your local market is likely to face a high vacancy rate or not, a good power team, along with doing your own due diligence, should show you the long-term economic outlook of the market you are shopping in.

Risk #3:
There Could Be Unforeseen Issues with the Property

Many new investors are afraid they may unwittingly buy a property that has hidden defects. This is why it's important to work with the proper professionals as part of your real estate power team.

A qualified and experienced property inspector will spot any problem areas, so you will know exactly what you are getting and how to deal with any defects that are found.

One smart way to minimize your risk is to negotiate the price of the property so that there is instant equity that will also help cover any of the repair costs. The better the deal you negotiate up front, the less risk you have of unforeseen problems.

And an astute real estate entrepreneur will always have a contingency fund put aside where a portion of the income from the property is allotted specifically to deal with any issues like this.

Risk #4:
Tenants Might Damage the Property

We have all heard horror stories about tenants from hell. As with most bad news, this tends to be the exception rather than the rule, but it's better to be prepared just in case.

Astute real estate entrepreneurs will handle this risk in several ways.

First of all, they will be rigorous in screening potential tenants, checking references, running credit and background checks, etc.

There is usually a damage deposit collected from the tenant prior to them moving into the property, which, in conjunction with a reserve fund, should cover any normal damage a tenant may cause.

And if the damage incurred is substantial, it should be covered by the property insurance.

If things are done properly in the first place, this particular concern should not cause you to lose any sleep.

This is particularly true if you are the money partner in the deal and you are working with an experienced, astute real estate entrepreneur.

Risk #5:
Something Catastrophic Might Happen to the Property

While no one can predict the future with any certainty, chances are you will go through your entire life without having any kind of fire, flood, earthquake, tornado, or other major disaster hit any of your rental properties.

That said, if something unpredictable does happen, that's what property insurance is for: to cover unexpected events. When you are properly insured, you will not only have your damages taken care of, but will also receive compensation for loss of rental income.

Risk #6:
Things Might Not Work Out between the Real Estate Entrepreneur & the Money Partners

There is no guarantee that the relationship between the real estate entrepreneur and the investor will always go smoothly. That's why it is so important that you know, like, and trust the person with whom you are working.

That said, if there is some sort of an issue, there should be an escape mechanism in the contract, allowing you to exit the deal without ruinous financial consequences.

Make sure to get proper independent legal advice and have a good contingency plan before entering into any partnerships.

Chapter 6 Summary:

So there you have it: six of the biggest risks and concerns people have about real estate investing, as well as tips on how to protect yourself.

If the property or rental market goes down, unforeseen issues with the property crop up, tenants damage the house, a disaster strikes, or you have problems with your money partners, there are always solutions to either prevent or mitigate your losses.

If anything in this chapter is unclear or you would like more information, please contact the author. Their contact infor- mation is on the back cover of this book. Speaking of questions and clarity, in the next (and final) chapter, we will go through the most frequently asked ques- tions people have about investing in real estate—especially as a money partner.

"It's tangible, it's solid, it's beautiful. It's artistic, from my standpoint, and I just love real estate."
Donald Trump

"A funny thing happens in real estate. When it comes back, it comes back up like gangbusters."
Barbara Corcoran

There are many questions that usually come up about
doing 'no sweat' deals...

Chapter 7:

Real Estate Investing FAQs

B y now, you should have a strong basic understanding of the pros and cons of real estate investing.

Although we have done our best to cover everything, you may still have some questions. That's why this chapter is dedicated to bringing even more clarity to the subject—answering questions that potential money partners have prior to getting involved in this kind of investment.

You should pursue this investment opportunity *only* if you have all the information you
need and no doubts linger in your mind.

So let's get started.

Question #1:
How do I know my money is secure?

Answer: In most cases, you know your money
is secure because you are either registered
as the owner on title or you have appropriate legal documentation showing your
ownership interest in the property.

This is why it's very important for you to
have independent legal advice prior to getting into any kind of a deal.

Bottom line: If your name is on the title and
you have legal documents to back up your
ownership claims, then you are secure.

Question #2:
What if the market drops drastically?

Answer: If the real estate market that you are investing in goes down dramatically, experience and history show that it will rebound over time.

So if you are invested in a medium- to long-term buy-and-hold strategy, this should not be a problem. In the worst-case scenario, your investment timeframe may need to be extended by a year or two.

Question #3:
Can I use my retirement plan to invest in real estate?

Answer: In some cases you can invest your retirement funds into real estate, but it depends on how the deal was structured in the first place.

If you are not sure, please contact the author to find out more about the kind of

deals that are compatible with your retirement plan.

Question #4:
How involved am I, as a money partner, going to be in the deal?

Answer: The real estate entrepreneur is the
one who is doing the heavy lifting for you,
including finding the property, making
the offer, putting together the power team,
managing the whole transaction, and
maintaining the property.

Therefore, your involvement will be lim-
ited to providing the funds and/or credit,
as well doing your own due diligence to
make sure that you are comfortable with
the deal and the person with whom you
are investing.

Question #5:
Why should I choose real estate instead of other investment options?

Answer: By reading this book, you are becoming familiar with all the compelling advantages of investing in real estate. The first two chapters outline these points in detail.

If you are still thinking that there might be another investment opportunity out there that's better than real estate, consider this question: Can the other investment provide you with the same kind of potential returns, multiple profit centers, and security as a real estate deal?

If not, then real estate really is your best option.

Question #6:
How much money do I need in order to participate in your investment program?

Answer: It really depends on many factors including the size of the deal, the kind of strategy that is being followed, the price of the property, the market area the property is located in, the type of financing that is involved, how many investor partners are going to be involved, etc.

If you would like more information about the author's specific investment program and opportunities that are available, please use the contact information on the back cover of this book.

Question #7:
What is the timeframe for this investment? For how long will I have to invest?

Answer: Again, this depends on many factors, the main one being the type of deals you are focusing on. Please contact the author by using the contact information on the back cover to find out specifically what kind of strategy they focus on and what their investment timeline is.

Question #8:
I really want to invest, but I don't have a lot of cash handy to do it with. Can I still be involved?

Answer: Many people never get started in real estate because they think they have to have tens of thousands of dollars just sitting in the bank to invest. While that amount of savings would be nice, it's simply not in the picture for the average North American. The good news is that there may be other ways for you to gain access to the money you want.

If you have owned a home for a while, chances are you have unused equity in it. You could consider getting a home equity line of credit (HELOC) on your property and using that money to invest in other real estate deals.

If you have a registered retirement savings plan or 401K, you may be able to use those funds to invest in real estate. This may in- volve a bit of work at the beginning in order to get them switched over to a self-directed plan, but the returns and security you can have in real estate will make it very worthwhile.

If you have some cash available, and a friend or family member has some as well, you may consider joining forces with them and investing together.

As you can see, there are a variety of options available. Please contact the author to discuss your particular situation.

Question #9:
Real estate investing sounds great. Why don't I just do it myself?

Answer: If you want to do real estate investing all by yourself, that's fantastic. Hopefully, this book has given you encouragement and inspiration.

Before you go at it, however, learn as much as you can about all the tricks of the trade. Get properly educated. Take the time and invest the money in good training from a qualified expert in the real estate style you want to follow.

If, on the other hand, you would prefer a hassle-free, no-sweat style of investing, then being a money partner and working with an experienced real estate entrepreneur may just be the right thing for you.

The happy money partner, Bill,
watching the profits come in.

Conclusion:

T hank you very much for reading this book which, hopefully, you found to be educational and enlightening.

At this point, you have several choices.

You can **do nothing and hope for the best** when it comes to taking charge of your finances and creating a better, more comfortable, wealthier life for yourself and your loved ones.

Frankly, this is what the vast majority of people do. A recent study by a major North American bank showed that one-third of respondents polled were counting on winning the lottery for their retirement! More than likely, that's not going to happen. We are all responsible for our own financial well-being and we have to go out and make it happen for ourselves.

You can **become a real estate entrepreneur yourself**, and start finding properties, negotiating deals, and coordinating your own team to make money with revenue properties. If you have the time, interest, and dedication to do this, go for it! It can be very profitable and fun.

I highly recommend that you find a good training program and a mentor to learn from. Reinventing the wheel and learning from the school of hard knocks is much too expensive and time consuming.

Or you can **become a money partner** and enjoy all of the benefits of real estate investing, but without the hassles of doing it all yourself. You can join forces with a driven and experienced real estate entrepreneur. Then you can help each other reach your financial goals by working together and doing more deals than either of you could do on your own.

It's all about creating win-win deals.

If you would like to find out about the author's No-Sweat Real Estate Investment program, please see the contact information on the back cover.

Contact the author and set up a time to go over the program either in person or online. The presentation will be a concise explanation of how it all works.

The author will be happy to explain everything in detail and show you what strategy they focus on, the market in which they invest, how much the investment is, and the anticipated returns you can enjoy.

If, after seeing the presentation, you feel that it is not a right strategy for you at this time, no problem. There is never any pressure to invest.

On the other hand, if it does make sense to you, the author will show you what the next steps are and how to proceed.

Thanks for reading this book. May you, too, enjoy all the benefits and profits of no-sweat real estate investing!